First published in 1979

ISBN 0 7188 2436 9

Printed in Hong Kong

Christian's Journey

John Bunyan's *Pilgrim's Progress*

Retold by RHODA COULDRIDGE
Illustrated by ANNA COULDRIDGE

LUTTERWORTH PRESS
Guildford and London

Introduction

The man who wrote this story was born a long, long time ago. His name was John Bunyan.

Although John's mother and father were very poor they were able to send him to school. He learned to read and write, but he was a very naughty boy. Often he did not listen to what the teacher said.

One day his teacher was reading a Bible story. In a stern voice he said, 'Children who are naughty will be thrown into the fires of hell and the devil will be there waiting for them.'

This frightened the class, and John made up his mind to become a good boy, but as soon as school was over he forgot his fears. As he grew older he refused to go to church and said the Bible was too boring to read. He chose the wrong kind of friends and began to swear and to tell lies.

Once when John and his friends were standing outside a shop they began to argue and quarrel. The shopkeeper came out to them and said, 'You really are wicked; you are worse than anyone I have ever known.'

John was ashamed and again decided to lead a better life, but he soon forgot and went back to his old ways. Then he met a young lady and fell in love with her.

When they were married she often talked about her father and how he had tried to follow in the way of Jesus Christ. Gradually John began to see the things that were wrong in his own life. He started to read his Bible and other books that would help him.

One day he gave his heart to the Lord Jesus. His fears and his wicked ways were gone. John was so happy then that he had to tell others about Jesus Christ. He went to the villages near by and preached there. Many people listened to him, but some were angry. They did not like what they heard and because of this John was arrested and put into prison.

He still wanted to help those who were trying to find the way to God, and while he was in prison he wrote about a traveller who had some very exciting adventures. He called his book The Pilgrim's Progress, from this world to that which is to come.

The City of Destruction

CHRISTIAN'S JOURNEY

HE was standing in the road near his house; just an ordinary man with a great bundle like a rucksack on his back. He was reading a book and as he read he began to tremble and cry.

'Oh dear, oh dear,' he cried. 'What shall I do? Whatever shall I do?'

After a while he closed the book and went home. Looking sadly at his wife and his children he said, 'Oh my dears, I have some dreadful news for you. Our town, this place where we live and have our friends, is in great danger. It will be destroyed by a fire which will come from heaven. We shall all be burned to death unless we can find some way of escape.'

He began to shake and cry again. Then his wife said, 'My dear, I think you must be ill to say such strange things. Come and rest. Tomorrow you will feel better.' She made him a hot drink, and tried to comfort him but he only became more and more distressed.

After a day or two, Christian (that was his name) was no better and his wife was no longer kind and understanding. 'You are mad,' she said. 'Stop talking about such things. You are only frightening the children.'

But Christian kept on reading his book and worrying about the fate of his family, and indeed about all his friends and neighbours. Sometimes he took his book and went away into the fields to read quietly and to pray. He knew that a lot of wicked things went on in the town, but he did not know how to get away from it all. So he stood in the fields, reading and crying.

Then, through his tears he saw a man coming towards him. The man's name was Evangelist. (An evangelist is someone who teaches or explains the meaning of the words we read in the Bible.)

'Why are you crying?' asked Evangelist.

'I am afraid,' said Christian, 'I shall go to hell because of my wickedness.'

'Well,' replied Evangelist, 'stop crying and do something.'

'Do something,' repeated Christian. 'I don't know what to do. What shall I do to be saved?'

Evangelist pulled a rolled up piece of paper from his pocket and handed it to Christian. Christian opened up the paper and read out,

FLEE FROM THE WRATH TO COME.

'That's what I want to do,' he said. 'But how can I escape from an angry God?'

'Look,' said Evangelist. 'Do you see a little gate over there?'

Christian gazed across the field. 'No,' he answered, 'I can't see a gate.'

'Well then,' said Evangelist, 'can you see a shining light?'

'Yes, yes,' exclaimed Christian, 'I can see that.'

'Good. Now keep your eyes on that light,' said Evangelist. 'If you go towards it, you will see the gate. You must knock at the gate. It will be opened and you will be told what to do next.'

Christian was very excited when he heard these words. He began to run across the field.

From the door of their house his wife saw him running. 'Where are you going?' she shouted.

Then the children began to run after their father. 'Come back, don't leave us,' they cried.

The noise brought out some of the neighbours. They laughed and said, 'Let him go, he is mad.'

'Don't worry. We'll bring him back,' said one man.

'Yes, Mr Bendy-Pliable and I will go after him,' shouted Mr No-Bend Obstinate.

Quickly the two men ran into the field. Everybody was shouting. Christian put his fingers in his ears. He refused to listen. He would not even look back. He had his heavy bundle on his back, so Mr Bendy and Mr No-Bend soon caught up with him.

'Come back with us,' they begged.

'No,' said Christian. 'I cannot go back. The city where you live is a wicked place. It will be destroyed. You come with me to a better land.'

'What!' cried Mr No-Bend, 'and leave all our friends and possessions behind?'

'I am going to a place where real treasure is stored, where neither rust nor moths can spoil it. You can read about it in my book.' Christian held out his Bible.

'We don't want to read that,' said Mr No-Bend. 'We just want you to come back with us.'

Christian shook his head. 'No,' he declared. 'I

am not turning back.'

'Well, I'm not wasting time with this madman,' Mr No-Bend said angrily. 'Come along Mr Bendy, leave him alone.'

'Just a minute,' Mr Bendy-Pliable said, 'if what Christian says is true, perhaps we ought to go with him.'

'Now you are the stupid one,' laughed Mr No-Bend. 'Don't take any notice of his book.'

'My book is the Word of God,' cried Christian.

Mr No-Bend took Mr Bendy-Pliable's arm. 'Let's go back,' he said.

Mr Bendy looked at Christian. 'How do you know which way to go?' he asked.

'I met a man named Evangelist,' Christian explained eagerly. 'He told me to keep on towards that shining light until I see a little gate where I shall receive further instructions.'

'I will come with you,' said Mr Bendy-Pliable.

Mr No-Bend turned towards the town. 'You won't get me on such a foolish journey. I am going home,' he cried.

So Christian and Mr Bendy-Pliable went on together.

'I am so glad you have decided to come with me,' said Christian.

'Well,' said his companion, 'since I am to accompany you on this journey, tell me more about it.'

'I am not very good at explaining things,' said Christian, 'but let me read it to you from this book.'

Mr Bendy-Pliable listened carefully. 'Hurry,' he cried. 'I want to get there as soon as possible.'

'I can't go any faster,' sighed Christian. 'I have such a bundle on my back. It is the load of all my wicked ways.'

They were so busy talking that they forgot to watch the path, and suddenly they both fell into a muddy, boggy patch.

'Oh dear,' cried Mr Bendy-Pliable. 'Now, look at the state we are in. Look at my clothes all messy and dirty. This is truly a pond of despair. If we ever get out of it I know where I shall go—straight back home again.'

Christian did not reply. He was struggling in deep mud and his heavy burden made it hard for him to get his feet moving. Then he saw that Mr Bendy-Pliable was trying to climb on to the path

again, near the place where they had fallen in. Christian struggled on alone. The mud seemed to pull at his feet and the weight of his burden pushed him deeper into the slime. Slowly and fearfully he plodded on.

'I shall never get out of this' he thought sadly. He looked up to see how much further he had to go before reaching the rocky path again. It was then he saw a man with his hand stretched out to him.

'What are you doing in the Slough of Despond?' asked the man.

'Oh sir,' said Christian, 'I am on my way to the Heavenly City and I was not watching the path when I fell into the mud.'

'There are some stepping stones. You need not have fallen in,' said the stranger. 'Now, give me your hand and I will help you on to the path again.'

So Christian reached out his hand and felt himself being pulled out of the mud on to the solid rocky path. Mr Bendy-Pliable, who had scrambled out on the other side, was now running swiftly back home.

The rescuer would not let Christian thank him. 'My name is Helper,' he said with a smile. 'I am glad that I was here when you needed me.'

'Couldn't something be done about that boggy patch?' Christian asked.

'It is not easy,' replied Helper. 'You see even when we drain away the bad parts, some of the mud seems to seep out and spoil the good parts. You will be all right now if you keep on this road.'

□   □   □

ONCE again Christian set off towards the little gate, but he had not gone far when he saw someone else coming across the field. This was Mr Worldly-Wiseman. He lived in the village next to Christian's and had heard all about him. As he came close to Christian he said, 'I see you have been in the bog. It is a wonder you did not sink right down with a bundle like that on your back.'

'Actually,' said Christian, 'I am on my way to get rid of it.'

'Oh,' said Mr Worldly-Wiseman. 'In that case, let me give you some advice. First of all, you are on the wrong road. Take this turning and you will come to the Village of Morality. The folk there are decent and respectable. I have a great friend who lives in the first house. He will help you with your load. He is a clever chap, very kind and willing to do anything for anybody.'

Christian was really tired of carrying his burden, so he decided to take Mr Worldly-Wiseman's advice. 'After all,' he thought, 'if I get rid of this load I will be able to walk more quickly. Besides, Evangelist did not mention getting rid of my bundle. He just said, "Go towards the shining light, knock at the little door, and then you will be told what to do next."'

So Christian turned along the road which led to the Village of Morality. Soon he came to a steep, steep hill. There were big rocks, some of them jutting out so far that Christian thought they might topple over and crush him. He was walking very slowly and the bundle on his back seemed to be getting heavier all the time.

'I shall never reach the top,' he thought, and as he looked up he gasped in surprise for there was Evangelist standing a little way along the path. He looked sadly at Christian.

'How did you get here?' he asked. 'Did I not show you the way to go?'

Christian was ashamed. He began to make excuses. 'Yes, you did, but I thought I could get rid of my burden quicker if I came this way.'

'Listen to me once more,' said Evangelist. 'Do as I tell you and go towards the light. Do not take any notice of Mr Worldly-Wiseman's advice. If you continue on this path, your burden will become heavier, you will sink beneath its weight and you will die.'

'Oh dear,' cried Christian. 'What am I to do? Where shall I go?'

Then Evangelist helped Christian to his feet and led him to the right road again. This time Christian could see the shining light quite easily, and soon he found the door. Over the door was a large notice which said,

KNOCK, AND IT SHALL BE OPENED TO YOU

Christian read the notice, then he knocked loudly.

Christian knocks on the door

He knocked several times before the door was opened.

'My name is Goodwill,' said the man at the door. 'Who are you, and what do you want here?'

'I am a poor traveller bowed down beneath this burden of my own wickedness,' replied Christian. 'I was told to come here and knock. Please may I come in?'

'Certainly,' answered Goodwill. Then he opened the door a little wider and to Christian's surprise he took him by the hand and quickly pulled him inside. After shutting the door, Goodwill turned to Christian with a smile and said, 'I always give a pull to those who wish to come in. You see Satan is not far away and he will try to stop you entering. Now, come with me and I will show you where to go. Can you see a little narrow path?'

'Yes,' replied Christian. 'I see the narrow way, but there are many other paths too.'

'Never mind about the other roads,' said Goodwill. 'You just keep to the straight and narrow way. Go on until you meet my friend. His name is Interpreter and he will explain anything you do not understand. His is the first house you come

to. Just knock at the door.'

'Thank you,' Christian replied, then hopefully he looked at Goodwill. 'Could I get rid of my load here?' he asked.

Goodwill shook his head. 'No, I cannot take that off for you, but if you keep on this narrow way you will come to a place where your burden will fall off.'

☐　　☐　　☐

SO Christian went along the straight and narrow path, and soon he reached Interpreter's house. In answer to his knock, a man came to the door.

'Sir,' said Christian, 'the man at the gate told me to call here. He said you would show me things which will help me on my journey.'

Then Interpreter invited Christian into the house. 'I have many things to show you,' he said. 'I will try and live up to my name and explain everything in a language which you can understand.'

Lighting a candle, Interpreter held it up so that Christian could look at a picture on the wall.

'Remember all that you see here,' he said. 'This picture will help you to know the true Guide, because I am warning you now that you will meet some who will lead you on the wrong path.'

Christian followed Interpreter into a large room. It was very dusty, even the floor had a layer of dust on it. Interpreter called for someone to come and sweep the room. As soon as the man came in and began to sweep, clouds of dust flew into the air and Christian began to choke and cough. Quickly Interpreter called to a girl, telling her to bring some water. When she sprinkled it on the dusty floor, the man was able to sweep without causing discomfort to those in the room and soon the place was clean.

'Now,' said Interpreter, 'I will explain all this. The sweeper is the law, like a policeman who can tell you that you have done wrong, but cannot take the wrong away. He can only punish you. The girl who sprinkled the water on the dust is like Jesus Christ who comes to clean up your heart and remove the dirt of your wicked sinful ways.'

'What does this mean?' asked Christian. They

had come to a place where a fire was blazing fiercely. A man was trying to put out the fire by pouring on water, but it seemed as if this only made the flames leap higher than before.

'Ah,' said Interpreter. 'The fire is the flame of love which burns in your heart. The one who tries to put it out is Satan. Now come with me and you will see what is happening on the other side.'

Then Christian saw a man who was secretly pouring oil on to the fire. 'That is how Jesus Christ works in your heart,' said Interpreter, 'helping you so that the flame of love which you have for him will turn into a glowing fire.'

Interpreter showed Christian many other strange and interesting things. They went into a very dark room. When Christian's eyes got used to the gloom he saw a man sitting inside a big iron cage. He was very sad and miserable. He was in such despair that he did not even try to get out of the cage.

'Poor fellow,' said Interpreter. 'He just sits there in misery and will never reach the Heavenly City unless he makes a move to get out and on to the right path.'

Christian murmured his agreement. He had learned a lot from what he had seen in Interpreter's house. At last Interpreter showed him which way to take and he set off again on his journey.

Along one side of the path was a very high wall, and Christian walked along beside it, but there was not much to see and soon he grew weary beneath his heavy load. Then he thought about some of the things which he had seen in Interpreter's house. He remembered that only Jesus could take away the heavy load of sin.

Thinking about Jesus helped Christian to forget his burden and suddenly he reached the top of a hill and saw the cross of Jesus. As he looked at the cross, a wonderful thing happened. Christian's bundle fell off and rolled away down the hill. It rolled into a deep, deep hole and was gone for ever.

Christian was very happy then. His heart was full of joy and peace. He was so happy that tears came into his eyes. He just stood there looking at the cross of Jesus and crying for joy.

Then through his tears he saw three angels, all shining with light and love.

One of them said, 'Peace to you.'

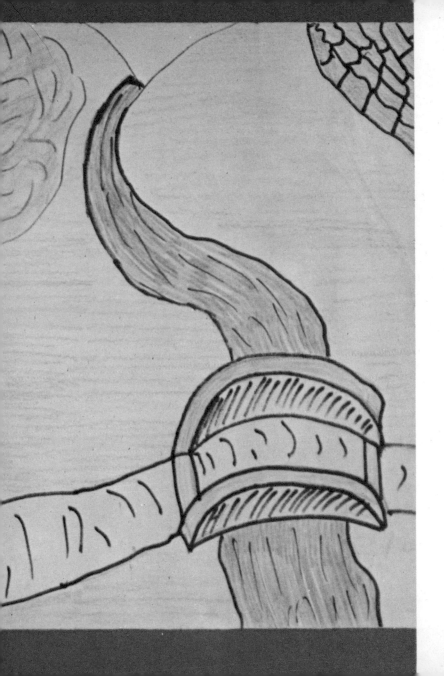

The second one said, 'Your sins are gone now. They are all forgiven.'

The third angel gave him new clothes and put a mark on his forehead. Then he handed him a scroll. 'Take care of this,' said the angel, 'because it will help you on your way. Also, you must hand it in when you reach the gates of the Heavenly City.'

Then they pointed out the way and Christian went on again. Without his burden he was able to travel faster, and down at the bottom of the hill he came upon three men who were fast asleep. Then he saw that they had chains round their ankles. Christian felt very sorry when he saw them. He shook them awake and offered to help them. He wanted them to share his happiness and he asked them to join him on his journey, but they were not interested.

One of them said, 'We are all right here. I don't see any danger.'

The second man yawned and said, 'I am too tired to walk with you. Let me sleep a little longer.'

The third one said, 'Don't worry about me. I'll soon catch up with you.'

23

Two men take a short cut
by climbing over the wall

Christian left them and turned to the path again. Then he saw two men climbing over the wall. When they saw Christian they hurried to catch up with him. Christian greeted them, then he said, 'Why did you not come here by the proper road, through the little gate as I did?'

'Oh,' they replied, 'that is a long way round. We took a short cut. Lots of people come over this way.'

'But,' said Christian, 'by coming in through the gate and keeping on the narrow path, I met with angels who gave me these clothes and put a mark on my forehead. Look.' He showed them his scroll. 'They gave me this. I have to show it when I get to the Heavenly City.'

The other two just laughed at Christian. They walked on together, but Christian did not talk to them. Sometimes he looked at his scroll and felt encouraged by the words he read.

Now the narrow path went up a great big hill. There was a little stream near by and Christian stopped to drink there.

□   □   □

AFTER drinking the cool clear water he felt refreshed and decided to attempt to climb the hill straight away. His two companions looked at the steep path and said they would try to find a way round the foot of the hill.

So Christian started up the Difficult Hill. He climbed, he scrambled, slipping, stepping over boulders, catching his feet in the tangle of ferns and heather. His hands and his feet were scratched and sore, and he panted so much that he thought he would never reach the top. About half-way up he found an arbour, a little sheltered spot where someone had put a seat. He was very thankful and sank down on the seat to rest. In fact he was soon fast asleep. He was so weary that his scroll fell from his hand, but he did not know this and he just slept on.

When Christian awoke he hurried on his way again. Just as he reached the top of the hill he met two men running towards him. Christian could see that they were two very frightened people.

'Whatever is the matter?' he cried. 'Stop! Stop! I believe that you are running in the wrong direction.'

Christian falls asleep in the arbour

'Indeed we are not,' said one of the men. He was shaking with fear.

'We were on our way to the Heavenly City,' the other man said, 'but there are two lions lying right across the road. We dare not go near them lest they tear us to pieces.'

'You make me scared too,' said Christian, 'but, I will go on, for I have been helped so much already, I am sure that I shall find courage to face even lions. Besides, I have a scroll which gives me fresh strength every time I read it.'

Christian felt for his scroll. It was gone! 'Oh dear,' he cried. 'Where is my scroll? Where can it be?'

Christian was very sad and he tried to think where he could have lost such a precious thing. 'I must find my scroll,' he said. 'I shall need it when I reach the Heavenly City.'

Leaving the two men, Christian ran swiftly back down the hill towards the sheltered place where he had stopped to rest. 'How stupid I am,' he said to himself. 'I have wasted time and energy by my carelessness. I could have been well on my way by now.'

Two frightened men
run back down the path

Back again at the little arbour Christian soon found his lost scroll. He picked it up and put it away safely.

Once more he went on his way, but not quite so joyfully as before. He kept thinking about the lions. 'Two fierce lions,' he said to himself. 'How am I going to get past them?' Then he cheered up as he said to himself, 'Maybe they're not there now.'

Christian looked anxiously along the road. To his surprise he saw a beautiful house, but before he could get to the house, there, right across the path, were two huge lions. The road was narrow and Christian was very frightened. His feet seemed rooted to the ground. He was afraid to go on. He was afraid to turn back. He did not know what to do.

Then he heard a voice which said, 'Don't be afraid. Don't you believe that God can help you?'

'Yes, yes. I do believe that,' said Christian, 'but the lions . . .'

Then the voice spoke again. 'Fear not. Believe that God can help you and the lions will not harm you.'

The lions roared loudly. Carefully, Christian walked right past them, and then he found that they were chained up, like a dog to a kennel. The chains were too short for the lions to reach Christian so they could not harm him.

When he was safely past the lions, a man came up to him. 'My name is Watchful,' said the stranger. 'Why are you so late?'

After Christian had explained that he had had to turn back and look for his lost scroll, Watchful took him to the Beautiful House and called to the lady who lived there. She asked about Christian's journey and when he had told her some of his adventures she invited him to spend the night in the Beautiful House. Then she introduced Christian to her three sisters whose names were, Prudence, Piety and Love. It was a happy time for Christian. The time went by very quickly as he sat with the sisters and talked of God's wonderful love.

The next morning the sisters took Christian to see the lovely view which they had from their house. 'See,' they said, 'over there are the Delightful Delectable Mountains. But there are many dangers

ahead. You must wear this suit of armour so that you will be safe.' Then the sisters gave Christian special protective clothing and a helmet, a shield and a sword.

When Christian left the sisters and the Beautiful House he had many things to think about. He wondered about the difficulties which he still had to face. 'In my armour and with my sword I shall be ready for anything,' he thought. So he sang as he went along.

□   □   □

SUDDENLY Christian saw a terrible monster coming across the field. He was very scared. Then he pulled his sword out of its sheath and his courage returned. He went on boldly to meet the awful creature. Then, to Christian's surprise the fearsome looking dragon greeted him and was quite friendly.

'My name is Apollyon,' he told Christian. 'I know where you are going and I would like to help you. I must warn you that there are many dangers on the way—perhaps you should go back now while you are still able. In any case, I know about the burden which you carried and which fell off and rolled into the bottomless pit. I am the angel of that bottomless pit and I know all about you. I know your sinful ways. In fact I know that you have been so wicked that you will never be allowed to enter the Heavenly City, even if you succeed in getting there.'

Christian nodded his head solemnly. 'What you say is true,' he said, 'but my sins are all forgiven, and I lost my burden at the cross of Jesus.'

When Apollyon heard the name of Jesus, he was very angry. Instead of being a smiling dragon he changed into a dreadful roaring creature, breathing out flames and fiery darts. Hastily Christian put up his shield of faith and using his strong sword of the Spirit, he began to struggle with Apollyon. It was a hard battle and Christian bled from his wounds, but in the end he won and the defeated Apollyon flew angrily away.

Once more the path was quiet and peaceful and Christian knelt down to thank God for helping him in the fight against the dreadful dragon. Then

Christian meets Apollyon

another exciting thing happened, for a hand appeared with leaves which came from the Tree of Life. When Christian put these on to his wounds they were healed immediately.

Well and strong again after the fight, Christian was able to continue his journey. He was walking along the narrow path again, when suddenly it led him downhill into a dark valley. It became so dark that Christian could hardly see, but he went on bravely although it was so frightening.

After a while, he almost bumped into two men who were running away from the darkness.

'Don't go any further,' they cried. 'It is pitch black down there. You cannot see anything at all, but you can hear howls and yells. There are dragons and wild beasts. There are goblins that pinch you. There are all sorts of horrible things.'

'This is the entrance to the Valley of the Shadow of Death,' said one of the men. 'Come back with us. If you go on, you will surely die.'

'I cannot turn back,' answered Christian. 'I was told to follow this path, and I believe that it is the way to the Heavenly City.'

He gripped his sword and although he could already hear strange noises in the darkness, he went steadily forward. Carefully he tried to feel the way with each step and discovered that there was a deep ditch at one side.

'If I fall into the ditch I shall never get out,' thought Christian. 'And if I fall into the bog on the other side of this narrow path I shall be lost for ever.'

Christian was trembling with fear and he lost all his courage. He stood still in the darkness and began to cry. Then some flames suddenly reached towards him through some big gates. Christian stared at the gates. He could see flames and smoke. Then he saw little groups of imps and devils. They were rushing to and fro. Some of them came right up to Christian and in the darkness he was afraid that he would fall down and be trampled on. But the most frightening thing of all was the groaning. Groans and cries from those who had gone through those big gates into hell.

Slowly, Christian went on. It was so dark everywhere. 'My sword is not enough for these dangers, he thought. 'Where can I find another weapon?'

Then his heart was filled with evil thoughts, for

Dragons and wild beasts prowl near the mouth of hell

A giant sits in
his cave near
some skeletons

some of the devils had come closer and were whispering wicked things into his ear. After a while Christian couldn't tell whether he heard these evil whispers or if he thought of such things himself. He was very distressed.

'I must not think such bad thoughts,' he said aloud. 'I will try to remember words of comfort from my Bible.'

Then he heard another voice which said, 'Even though I walk through the Valley of the Shadow of Death, I will fear no evil.'

The words and the voice brought peace to Christian. He knew now that he was not alone in the Valley. He became more courageous and tried to hurry so that he might catch up with other travellers. Little by little the valley grew lighter and soon Christian could see the path. He could also see lots of traps and nets along the way. Treading very carefully, he managed to pass them all in safety. He was very thankful to be in the daylight again and away from all the snares.

☐   ☐   ☐

FURTHER along the road Christian saw a giant sitting in a cave. Nearby was a skeleton. Christian kept to the narrow path and when he reached the top of the next little hill he saw someone walking on the road just a little way ahead of him.

'Why,' cried Christian in surprise, 'I know that man. It is Faithful. He comes from my own town.' Christian was very glad to find a companion and he shouted to Faithful to wait for him.

'I cannot wait,' replied Faithful. 'I must keep on my way.'

Then Christian began to run in order to catch up with Faithful. He even overtook him but suddenly he tripped over a stone and fell. Faithful helped Christian to his feet and they went on together, talking as they walked. Faithful told Christian how Mr Bendy-Pliable had returned to the town with the story of Christian's struggles in the bog.

'That was nothing compared with some of the things I have been through since,' said Christian. 'I was terrified in the Valley of the Shadow of Death. It was all so dark.'

'Dark!' exclaimed Faithful. 'It was lovely and

sunny when I came through.'

'In that case,' said Christian, 'you were spared a time of great terror, but look, over there, it seems we have a companion.'

The newcomer hastened to join Christian and Faithful. 'Hallo,' he said. 'My name is Talkative. I presume you are going to the Holy City. So am I. We might as well go on together.'

So now there were three travellers walking along the narrow way. Talkative was true to his name and talked most of the time. He was interesting to listen to even if he was not always correct in what he said. But soon, Christian and Faithful began to tire of his constant chatter.

'You certainly know your Bible,' said Christian after one of Talkative's long speeches, 'but do you know the Lord Jesus Christ?'

Talkative did not want to answer that question so he began to talk of other things. Christian and Faithful soon discovered that Talkative was no help to them and they decided to leave him. So the two friends walked on together and Talkative went on his way alone.

Looking back to see where Talkative was, Faithful saw someone else hurrying after them. It was Evangelist, and both Christian and Faithful were very happy to see him again.

'You are making good progress,' said Evangelist, 'but you must beware of the dangers which you will find all around you when you reach the town of Vanity Fair.'

There was no other way for Christian and Faithful to go, except through the town. It was a very noisy place. There was a great crowd of busy people, all shouting and jostling. There were beggars, thieves, cheats, jugglers, and side-shows of various kinds. There were traders shouting and trying to sell their goods. There were processions and other types of carnival fun.

When Christian and Faithful refused to stop and join in the fun the traders and the townspeople became very angry. They joked about the way Christian and Faithful were dressed. They laughed at their words and finally took them prisoner. Then Christian and Faithful were put into a cage and people came to see them locked up and to jeer at them.

The man in charge of the Fair was called Mr

A crowd watching
a joker doing his tricks

Hate-Good and the people of the town asked him to be judge and to decide what was to be done with the prisoners.

'This stranger,' said Mr Hate-Good, pointing to Faithful, 'has stirred up trouble by trying to bring truth and honesty into our town. Let him be beaten and stoned and then burnt to death.'

The crowd surged forward, seized Faithful, and attacked him with sticks, stones and knives. Then they tied him to a wooden stake, piled firewood around it and set it alight.

Poor Christian could not help and had to watch his friend's cruel death. He was very sad, when suddenly he saw behind the crowd a chariot and horses. He heard the sound of trumpets and to his astonishment Faithful was taken up into the Heavenly City.

After a while Christian managed to escape from the cage. As he was running away from the town a man from Vanity Fair ran after him and asked if he could go with him to the Heavenly City.

'My name is Hopeful,' said the man. 'I am sorry that we killed your friend. I know now that he was a good man. I heard him speak about the

Christian and Faithful are put in a cage

Mr By-ends and his friends

Lord Jesus, and when I saw how brave he was I have been thinking very much about my own wicked ways. May I go with you to the Heavenly City?'

So, Christian and Hopeful walked on together, and further along the road they met a man called Mr By-ends. He greeted the two friends and told them that he came from the town of Fair-speech.

'Some of my friends are just over there,' he said, and introduced Christian and Hopeful to three other men, Mr Money-love, Mr Save-all and Mr Hold-the-World.

These were all clever men who had learned how to get what they wanted by telling lies, or flattering people. They had even used violence. Sometimes they pretended to be followers of Jesus Christ. It did not take Christian and Hopeful long to find out they were not the kind of friends they wanted to walk with.

They soon left them behind and continued happily on their journey, sharing each other's friendship.

□   □   □

FOR most of the way the narrow road had taken them up and down steep hills, but at last there were no hills in sight and they could see right across the fields. They crossed the lovely fields and entered the Plain of Ease. There were all kinds of flowers and a pretty little stream with a bridge across it. It was a really peaceful place. Christian and Hopeful were able to sit down and rest and forget all their fears and worries.

After a short rest, Christian and his friend wandered happily over the grassy path. Soon they reached a place where there were some silver mines. As they drew near one of the miners called out and invited them to visit the mines.

'Thank you,' replied Christian, 'but we cannot stop to see the silver mines. We must keep on our path.'

'Oh do come!' said the man. 'Silver is a valuable mineral. You could become rich. There is surely nothing wrong in that?'

'No, indeed,' answered Christian. 'It is not wrong to be rich, but the love of money is the root of evil. We are seeking God's way and we shall not turn aside even to look at the mines. Many people have lost their way by doing just that.'

At that moment Mr By-ends and his friends arrived. They decided it would be fun to visit the mines, and it would not take them far out of the way. Christian and Hopeful left the others and continued on the grassy plain. Just beyond the mines they saw a signpost. It pointed back towards Vanity Fair. Another arm showed the way to By-path Meadow and in the other direction was the Straight and Narrow Way.

After a short rest Christian and Hopeful followed the Narrow path. It was rough and stony, and they looked longingly at the lovely grassy footpath over the field. Then Christian said, 'These paths seem to go side by side, surely if we walked on the grass we should be all right.'

Then they climbed over a stile and saw a man who was also walking on the grassy path. Christian stopped and asked if they were on the right road for the Heavenly City. The man's name was Mr Know-All.

'Yes,' he said. 'This is right. Besides you can see the other road from here, so you can't go wrong.'

He seemed quite certain that it was the right

Christian and Hopeful enjoy
walking in the Plain of Ease

A storm blows up with bursts of thunder and flashes of lightning

road, so Hopeful and Christian decided to follow Mr Know-All.

Soon it grew quite dark. Black clouds blotted out the sunshine. A heavy storm blew up with loud bursts of thunder and bright flashes of lightning. Christian and Hopeful were lost. They tried to follow Mr Know-All who was a little way ahead. Suddenly they saw him stumble. He had fallen into a deep pit and was killed as he fell.

Christian and Hopeful did not know which way to go. 'Perhaps we should go back to the stile and see if we can find the Narrow Way again,' said Christian. Hopeful agreed, so they turned back but they could not find the place where they had climbed over. They did find a little shelter, so decided to stay there until the storm was over.

☐   ☐   ☐

SAFE in the shelter, they made themselves comfortable and were soon fast asleep. Alas, the shelter was in the grounds of a big castle which was owned by a Giant called Despair.

Every morning when the Giant awoke he got up and took an early morning stroll. When he found Christian and Hopeful in his shelter he captured them and took them back as prisoners to his Castle of Doubt and Unbelief. The two friends were thrown into a dark dungeon, and were not given anything to eat or drink. They were very unhappy and they began to despair of ever reaching the Heavenly City.

Christian was very sorry. 'It is all my fault,' he said. 'I persuaded you to leave the Narrow Way.'

'Perhaps we can escape,' said Hopeful.

Then the Giant sent his servant to punish the trespassers and they were beaten until they could hardly stand.

'We shall die here,' said Christian. 'I would rather kill myself than face another beating from the Giant.'

Hopeful tried to comfort him. 'God has helped us so far. Surely he will not forsake us now,' he said.

'You are right,' answered Christian. 'Let us pray about it.' As he mentioned prayer, Christian's face lit up with joy. 'I have just remembered,' he cried

Giant Despair captures the travellers

excitedly. 'I have a key called Promise which will open any lock in Doubting Castle.'

'Why, of course, how could we forget the Promise of God?' said Hopeful.

So without any difficulty, Christian and Hopeful were able to get out of the Giant's Castle with the special key—God's Promise.

Once outside the Castle they soon found their way back to the stile where they left a warning to help others.

Their path now led into the Delightful, Delectable Mountains. Everywhere was beautiful The gardens were lovely. Christian and Hopeful ate some of the fruit from the trees. There were streams of clear water where they were able to refresh themselves.

After a good wash they both felt much better. They climbed higher up the mountain path and stopped to talk with some shepherds who were tending their sheep. Christian asked if they were on the right path for the Heavenly City.

'Oh yes,' the shepherds said. 'These are the Delightful, Delectable Mountains. You are still a long way off, but if you look over there you will be able to see the City.'

Christian and Hopeful were very happy to have their first glimpse of the Heavenly City and they wanted to hurry on and get there as quickly as possible.

'You must watch where you are walking,' said the shepherds. 'You cannot hurry over the hills. If you fall over the edge there is a very steep drop on one side.'

Then Christian and Hopeful followed the shepherds and peeped over the cliff. They both gasped with horror when they saw a pile of bones and skulls lying far below.

'That is the Hill of Error,' said the shepherds. 'If you make a mistake you could end up at the bottom as these people did. There is a hill called Caution too, and there you will see people stumbling about. They are blind. You managed to escape from Giant Despair, but they did not. The wicked Giant put out their eyes and then led them to the hill where they wander about unable to find the Way.'

One of the other shepherds then showed Christian and Hopeful a door which led into the third hillside.

Shepherds tend their sheep in the Delightful Delectable Mountains

They see into hell

He opened the door and called the travellers to look inside. Christian and Hopeful could smell burning and they could hear groans and cries.

'What does this mean?' Christian asked fearfully.

'It is another entrance into hell,' replied the shepherd.

'Did all these people set off to find the Heavenly City?' asked Hopeful.

'Yes,' the shepherd sighed. 'There are many who set off, and there are many who fall away.'

Then they saw a man who had been tied up with seven ropes by seven devils. The devils were carrying him back through the door into hell.

'Take care that you keep on the right path,' warned the shepherd, 'because there is no escape from hell.'

Before Christian and Hopeful left to continue their journey, the shepherds gave them more warnings.

'Don't be led astray by Mr Flatterer when you meet him. And mind you do not sleep on any enchanted ground,' they said.

Then Christian and Hopeful said goodbye and went on their way.

52

Christian and
Hopeful see
a man who has been tied up with
seven ropes by seven devils

REMEMBERING all that they had seen and heard they walked carefully, but had not gone very far when they met up with a man who was very polite and friendly. His clothes were clean and white, but underneath his nice clothes he had a black, wicked heart. This was Mr Flatterer. He was such a nice man, that Christian and Hopeful forgot the shepherds' warning.

Mr Flatterer said, 'I can see that you are good men, and I would like to help you to reach the Holy City. This is the best way to go. Follow me and you will be quite safe.'

Christian and Hopeful decided to follow him, but Mr Flatterer was not telling the truth and before long he led them into a net where they got themselves all tangled up. Then Mr Flatterer lost his white robe, and Christian and Hopeful were able to see his black heart. They knew then that they had been following the way of Satan.

They could not get out of the net and they began to cry. How they wished that they had taken more notice of all that the shepherds had told them. While they were struggling in the net a Shining Angel came to them. He was carrying a whip.

'What are you doing in this net?' the Angel asked. 'Didn't the shepherds tell you not to listen to Mr Flatterer?'

'Yes, the shepherds did warn us,' said Christian and Hopeful, 'but we forgot!'

Then the Angel helped them out of the net and said to them, 'So, you forgot!' Raising his whip, the Shining Angel beat them both. 'Now,' he said, 'next time, remember all that you have been told.' After he had whipped Christian and Hopeful, the Angel went away.

Christian and Hopeful walked on together, this time taking great care to keep on the right path. When they met a man coming in the opposite direction who begged them to return with him, they would not listen to his arguments. Not even when he kept on saying, 'I am turning back. Let me tell you this—there is no such place as the Heavenly City. There is no God. I have been all the way over the mountain and I have not had one glimpse of the Holy Place.'

Christian and Hopeful turned away from this unbeliever, and keeping on the narrow path they came to a place where the air seemed hot and heavy. Their steps became slower, and at last Hopeful said, 'Oh Christian, I feel so sleepy, let us stop and rest. I am sure I shall feel better after a little nap.'

'No, no,' cried Christian. 'We dare not sleep here. I am sure it is the enchanted ground which the shepherds spoke about.'

Then Hopeful remembered, but his eyes were heavy and he was almost asleep when Christian said sternly, 'Look, Hopeful, I am sleepy too, but we have to keep walking, and if we talk as we walk we shall keep each other awake.'

So they began to talk, each one telling how he came to be on the road to the Heavenly City. They talked about how wonderful everything would be when they reached the end of their journey. Then they found that they had left the enchanted ground behind them and had come to a place called Beulah-land. Everything was so beautiful; there was no night there, only sunshine.

As Christian and Hopeful walked on they saw the gardener. He came up to them and showed them a place where they could rest. Christian and Hopeful went into the shelter and slept.

56

They rest in
the beautiful
garden

The gardener points to
the Heavenly City
and shows them
many wonders

When they awoke, they felt much better and were ready to continue their journey. There were birds singing, lovely flowers, and happiness everywhere. Best of all they could see the Heavenly City before them shining like gold. But, between them and the end of their journey, there was a wide, fast-flowing river.

'You must walk right through the water,' said the gardener. 'There is no bridge and no boat to take you across.'

Standing on the river bank, Christian and Hopeful looked at the swirling water. It looked so swift and so cold. The friends hesitated, fearful again.

'Is the water very deep?' asked Christian.

'You will find it very deep in some places,' replied the gardener. 'In fact, you will find it deep or shallow according to the amount of faith which you have in the King of the Heavenly City.'

Then Christian and Hopeful stepped bravely into the water. Immediately Christian began to sink. 'Help,' he cried. 'The waves are going right over my head.'

Hopeful reached out and tried to support his friend. 'Come, my dear Christian,' he said, 'it is

not deep here, my feet are on the bottom.'

Then Hopeful encouraged Christian to walk towards the middle of the river. 'Remember,' he urged, 'remember what Jesus said. "Do not be afraid. Trust in me."'

Poor Christian was so frightened that he would have been swept away and drowned but for Hopeful's strong arm.

'I shall never reach the other side,' groaned Christian.

'Yes, you will,' said Hopeful. 'There is a place there for you. The King has promised us that. He said, "I have prepared a place for you, and I will be there to meet you." He will hold you fast.'

These words helped Christian to go on, and keeping his thoughts on the Heavenly King, he managed to struggle through the water and found his feet upon the solid rock. As they drew nearer to the other side of the river they saw two Shining Angels standing on the bank. The Angels reached out to help Christian and Hopeful and lifted them safely out of the water. With the two Shining Angels to support them Christian and Hopeful went quickly up the hill to the gates of the Heavenly City.

There they saw one of the men whom they had met during their journey along the Narrow Way. He was being turned away from the gates of gold and pearl because he had no scroll to show. Christian was glad then that he had kept his scroll carefully, in spite of many dangers and adventures. Hopeful, too, was welcomed into the Holy City, and although he did not have a scroll he was allowed to enter because of his true belief and faithfulness to the King of the Heavenly City.

Christian and Hopeful gazed at each other in joy as they saw that they had become like the Shining Ones. Other Shining Angels came to welcome them and lead them into the City. Christian and Hopeful joined with them in singing,

GLORY, GLORY TO THE ONE WHO SITS UPON THE THRONE.

Immediately, bells began to chime. More Shining Angels came with harps and there was great gladness everywhere as Christian and Hopeful entered the Heavenly City in triumph.

Christian and Hopeful enter
the Heavenly City in triumph